D-Day 60th Anniversary
NORMANDY LANDINGS
A 19-year-old's diary with unique photos

W B Carter

D1609740

ATHENA PRESS
LONDON

ISBN 1 84401 266 2

First Published 2004 by
ATHENA PRESS
Queen's House, 2 Holly Road
Twickenham TW1 4EG
United Kingdom

Printed for Athena Press

D-Day 60th Anniversary
NORMANDY LANDINGS
A 19-year-old's diary with unique photos

By the same author:

Saved by the Bomb
D-Day Landings

Foreword

Sixty years after the event, perhaps the most amazing feature of D-Day is the sheer scale of the operation. From the sea and the air, 156,000 Allied troops landed in Normandy, and 195,000 personnel were involved in Operation Neptune (the naval assault crossing). These numbers alone tell only half the story.

D-Day could not have taken place without the work of thousands of men and women, from dockyard hands to the NAAFI, acting in support of the frontline services. Yet on 6th June 1944, the burden fell upon those men – the sailors, soldiers and airmen, Royal Marines, merchant seamen and others – who were operating off the Normandy coast or in the air, who ran up beaches, or dropped from the sky by parachute or glider. They had the task of making D-Day a success.

Without their efforts, courage and sacrifices, the Normandy landings would have failed.

Faced with the enormity of D-Day, this book is a valuable reminder that each of those people taking part in the landings was an individual human being. Each had their own experiences that day, their own fears for what was to come, their own hopes for the future.

For many of the individuals, the war forever altered the course of their lives. W B Carter's unusual photographs and detailed recollections bring home the experiences of one of those who was directly involved in the centre of the landing operations.

Sixty years on, this book is an excellent way to remember the Normandy landings.

Andrew Whitmarsh
Military History Officer
D-Day Museum

Sub Lieutenant Brian Carter RNVR

Preface

Whilst there have been numerous books written about Operation Overlord, better known as D-Day, there are few – if any – giving personal accounts of experiences in the actual landings. The majority of landing craft after beaching would return to the UK to pick up another load. A few craft, however, were detailed to offload the many ships that had anchored within the harbour. They worked relentlessly night and day ferrying troops, vehicles etc., which were needed to support our invading forces.

As a teenager, nineteen to be exact, second in command of a landing craft, I have described here the many landings that we undertook, illustrated with photos taken by myself. An enormous strain was put on the crew who went many days without any rest, the craft being finally destroyed in the great storm that followed. Inaccuracies in small details may appear, since the book is written purely from memory. A very few of the events portrayed occurred on other craft, but are included in order to give as true and interesting a picture as possible of events which occurred over many landings on that fateful shore.

Introduction

When I walked into the first training establishment I was extremely nervous. All naval establishments had 'HMS' in front of their names. This was important for those joining up in order to familiarise them with naval terms; for instance, when we left the establishment it would be termed 'going ashore'.

Right from the start we came under very stern discipline, which I found no problem, for at school from the age of fourteen we had to spend two afternoons of the week doing OTC – Officers' Training Corps – so I was well used to discipline and the handling of small arms. I wonder why so much fuss was made over the Hitler Youth, when in fact I had received military training, with many others, from such an early age.

I was picked out to be CW candidate. This stood for 'Commissioned Warrant' – to be trained as a naval officer, and get a commission, providing I passed all the various courses that I was sent on during the next few months. First I went to HMS *Glendower* at Pwllheli which had been a Butlins holiday camp for my initial training, and then a month at sea on a light cruiser, HMS *Diomede*, to be followed by a short course at Lancing College, and finally ending at HMS *King Alfred,* situated in the underground car park at Hove!

In those four months we had to learn Morse code, signalling by flags, seamanship, navigation, knots and splices, gunnery, aircraft recognition, and the rudiments of ship handling. All these courses were extremely hard, and continued late into the evenings. We only had Saturday afternoons off. This put us under considerable stress, which was not helped by a bad outbreak of food poisoning at one of the camps, and most of us, when it came to our final exams, were suffering from stress and many had tummy troubles.

We had started off as being 240 CW candidates, and now were down to less than 100, when the day came when we would all assemble in the drill hall and be told whether we had passed. Opposite the car park, tailors' shops had sprung up to serve the navy only, so that every candidate had his uniforms made directly. Thus, when anyone had passed they could immediately obtain their uniforms and all the necessary gear, including a suitcase, without delay. In the event of someone not getting a commission, it was just bad luck for the tailor's shop.

The Captain of HMS *King Alfred* read out the names of those who had passed, and my heart sank when my name was not called. Even though we had not passed all our exams, those who had failed could go before a Board of Admirals to be interviewed, and might still be granted a commission. There were about a dozen of us queuing outside the Admirals' office. The first two who went in came out in tears, having been failed. I was next to go in and boldly stood in front of the board. One of the admirals was one of my mother's cousins. However, in no way was I going to mention this, and after one admiral had asked me a few questions he said, 'I think you are the type we need, Carter.' So I had passed. What a relief!

I rushed across the road to get my uniforms and found to my horror that the shop was shut. There was no point in them being open once they had thought everyone had collected their uniforms. Fortunately, the adjacent shop was open and they kindly got in touch with a staff member of the shop where I had ordered my uniforms, and without much delay they opened up. I then hurried back to the camp to get dressed and ready for the passing out parade.

It is difficult to describe the load that had been lifted from my mind, for had I failed I would have been drafted to a ship as an ordinary seaman; and after my short experience on a light cruiser, I would not have liked again to serve on the lower deck. It was Christmas 1943, six months since I joined up, and never did I think that in six months' time I would be landing on the beaches of Normandy. We were granted two weeks leave and told we would receive orders as to where we would be drafted. I spent my leave visiting relations and the firm where I had worked. I had been in a reserved occupation, and whilst my boss had tried to keep me on, I went against his wishes and joined up.

I could not help but wonder when my orders would come, and where I was to be sent, and oddly enough was extremely eager for my leave to end. When my orders arrived I was told to report to Troon, which was the headquarters for landing craft, and it took little imagination to realise that one was going to take part in Operation Overlord, better known today as D-Day.

Those who started the course.

Those who passed the course.

Training for D-Day

My previous journey to Scotland as a seaman was horrendous. We had to stand most of the way, stopping at a few stations where voluntary workers would provide us with sandwiches, and the sailors would go to the bar, many being extremely drunk by the end of the journey. However, as an officer I managed to get a seat in a first class carriage, and when I arrived I was told that due to an epidemic of dysentery at Troon I was to go as an additional officer on a landing craft Mark IV which was fully commissioned and engaged in practice landings, getting the crew fully trained for their various duties. Whilst on most LCT Mark IVs, all the officers had to live and sleep in the very small wardroom, but on a few there were two cabins on what was called the 'troop shelter', so that I had the wardroom to myself as far as sleeping was concerned. The Skipper made me very welcome, and that evening decided that he and the First Lieutenant would go ashore, which they had never been able to do before, as it was always necessary to have one officer on board.

The landing craft were moored in trots, which were wooden structures each spaced slightly longer than a landing craft, so that craft could moor with their bows attached to one structure and their stern to the other. This allowed a large number of craft to be accommodated in a very efficient way. Liberty boats would steam from one end to the other picking up those who were going ashore, and also delivering mail.

The signalman came into the wardroom with a signal saying that we were to water ship, which meant leaving our mooring and tying up alongside a barge to fill our water tanks. I hesitated about what to do, and summoned the coxswain and explained the situation and the fact that I had no experience of handling a landing craft. My boating experience had been confined to a rowing boat on Derwent Water, and a few hours trying to learn ship handling at Portslade on a small harbour launch. The engines were started, ropes cast off and without much difficulty I managed to berth alongside the water barge, and to my horror saw there was just an old man who had to fill our tanks by hand with a semi-rotary pump. By the time he had finished it was starting to get dark, and I decided that I would sail the craft up to the trot so that they could secure the bow, and then go astern so that they could get a rope around the aft trot. I came in slowly and managed to get the bow rope secured, but then the tide started to pull the stern round and there was no way I could overcome this with the engines. I therefore decided to do what pilots are told, and that is if you are doing a bad landing, abort and come in again. This time, after a bit of thought, I realised the tide could well be made use of, so I came in the other way round against the tide, the bow rope secured, the stern drifting nicely back on to the aft trot, and we berthed without any problems.

I had learnt my first lesson: always, when possible, make use of the tide or wind – whichever is the stronger – when mooring up. I sat back in the wardroom feeling quite pleased with myself, and giving my blood pressure a chance to subside.

It was dark when the liberty boat arrived with the Skipper and First Lieutenant, and even though the former had enjoyed some heavy drinking in the local pub, he noted that the ship was moored a different way round to when he left. I showed him the signal and said that the craft had been duly watered. He was horror struck, and said the craft should never be moved without there being two officers on board! However, he was not cross with me and I think he was secretly pleased, for if I had not carried out the order he might have been in trouble for leaving the craft with his First Lieutenant, with theoretically no officer on board, for I think his was the only craft to have been given an extra officer as a temporary arrangement.

The craft had not been long commissioned, and we were engaged on practice beachings being part of a flotilla of twelve craft. A lot of practice was needed, for the craft would steam in line abreast towards a beach and drop their anchors that were at the stern about 40 yards before landing on the beach. If one dropped one's anchor too soon, then the cable would have run out before landing, giving one only two options, one to haul in the anchor and thereby pull the craft away from the beach, or in action one would have had to cut the cable and land. The idea of dropping the anchor was to keep the craft bow-on to the beach, and also to help pull it off having unloaded.

On each side of the bow were two winch shelters. Two men would man each winch and drop the door when ordered. Having unloaded, they would pull up the door as quickly as possible, as the door itself gave good protection against small arms fire. The two oerlikon guns would each be manned by two seamen, the coxswain would be on the wheel and a signalman on the bridge. The First Lieutenant would be on the tank deck. It was his job when the door had been dropped to rush forward with a pole to ascertain the depth of the water into which the tanks or vehicles had to drive. This was a somewhat suicidal task if the craft was under fire.

Problems would be encountered if the tide was dropping fast, so it was imperative to unload as quickly as possible. Not only did we practise unloading but also evacuating troops and tanks from beaches, and on one occasion we found ourselves loaded up with troops but firmly stuck on the beach. I suggested that we got all the troops on to the stern of the craft and get them to jump in unison. After about half a minute the craft started to dip at the stern and the bows come up, and with the engines going full astern and hauling on the anchor, we managed to get off. The Skipper was summoned the next day, thinking he was going to get into trouble, but he was congratulated on the initiative he used in getting the troops to jump.

Sometimes the landings would go off without a hitch, but if there was a bad crosswind, occasionally one craft would drop its anchor cable over another, causing chaos. However, for all that we were learning, and I myself gained considerable experience which proved invaluable later on. Night landings were also practised, and it was somewhat difficult, particularly when we had an army officer on the bridge, to stop them interfering, for one needed all one's concentration to judge the distance one was from the beach at night.

Returning from these exercises we sometimes moored up alongside a jetty, and I was not impressed by the way the Skipper handled the craft, or the way the crew secured us when we came alongside.

One evening before we were due to take part in a night landing the Skipper sent me on to the bridge to send a signal by Aldis lamp to the shore. Morse code takes a long time to learn, and I could only manage it at a somewhat boy scout speed. When one signals, one first indicates that one has a message to send, and after each word, if the person the other end has understood it, he then sends back a flash. One then proceeds with the next word, and again after each word one gets a flash, and a series of flashes indicate the end of the message. Whilst I managed to send out a signal, when it came to the reply, it was far too fast for me, and the person sending it must have thought I was a complete clot. However, from then onwards, in the evenings, I used to spend time reading messages that were going to and fro between other ships, and within about six months I was able to read Morse almost as quickly as I could talk.

We also had been taught semaphore, which I found much easier, and also how to read flags, the flags each indicating a letter of the alphabet. The message would not be spelt out in full, but referenced to a series of signal hoists; generally a sequence of three flags would indicate one's message. As the flags were hoisted on a mast, one had reasonable time to refer to the list of signals. These would be fairly standard, such as 'permission requested to go alongside', 'medical assistance required when I land', 'I request assistance of a tug' and many other signals. After about three weeks the dysentery had been overcome at Troon. I was put on a gunnery course, where we had to learn aircraft recognition, gunnery and various procedures with regard to landing craft which had not been covered in our original training. Oddly enough, when it came to the exams I passed with top marks. It was somewhat strange to be first in the gunnery course but last in the CW training, particularly in view of the fact that I was useless at aircraft recognition! The training in aircraft recognition was done in a large blown-up balloon-shaped tent where various aircraft would be shown by a projector onto the fabric above us. This was quite a clever idea, for it was far better than seeing a model of a plane put in front of you.

A practice landing

My Landing Craft for D-Day

I received orders to join an LCT Mark V moored on the Clyde where they had been unloading American landing craft and getting them into commission. D-Day was getting very close, and most of the craft had proceeded down to the south coast, but the craft that I was allocated had been a problem one, and for some reason had partly submerged – why, I never knew – and it required a considerable amount of work to get it operational. It had been left until last, and due to the fact it was vital to have as many landing craft as possible, it was de-watered and commissioned.

The Skipper and I were the first to arrive. We were living in a hotel at the time. Various defects kept coming to light. The crew arrived and it turned out that they had all been together on another craft, which proved to be an unwise move, for when ships are decommissioned it was always the normal practice to send the crew on different ships to avoid the problem that we had of the crew saying how they did things differently on their last ship. There is an expression in the navy, 'Different ships, different long splices'. In other words, skippers have their own way of going about their duties, one way just as good as the other. The Captain always has his own standing orders, which must be obeyed. Some would be fairly lax and allow smoking when on duty providing it was not in the engine room, where others would forbid it outright. It was generally sensible to allow smoking, otherwise seamen would spend a long time in the heads having what was known as 'a spit and a draw'.

My job as First Lieutenant proved extremely difficult and I had a lot to learn with regard to establishing discipline. I soon learnt that if one let a crew member off for creating some misdemeanour, when it was repeated by another member of the crew one would feel they had to let him off with a good 'bottling'. It was far better to punish the offender, for the crew would then realise that you stood no nonsense. One of the most common problems was a quartermaster sleeping when on watch, for when in harbour or at anchor at night there would only be one man on duty, in sole charge of the safety of the craft.

In order to get the ship fully in commission we had to draw all the necessary stores, etc. This meant going to Rosyth in a van, and going to each of the very large buildings to obtain the necessary gear and stores. As ours was a very small ship, the store attendants were never very helpful, particularly when it came to food and having to break up a crate. The major problem we had was that there were no sets of American spanners available, English ones being completely useless on an American ship, so that the engineer had to make do with adjustable spanners and Stillson wrenches. This, with the engines giving perpetual trouble, made his work almost impossible at times.

At last we sailed. We found ourselves flotilla leader, with eleven other craft of various types, and set sail for Dartmouth. With only two officers, we had to do four hours on and four hours off, which was extremely tiring, for having done our four hours on the bridge, we then had all the various duties with regard to the running of the ship to supervise. The responsibility of leading the flotilla fell hard on our shoulders, for I had never been solely in charge of a ship during the day, let alone at night. There were no buoys or lighthouses to help us, and the first night we had a signal from the shore saying we were steaming through a minefield. Fortunately the craft drew very little water, so we came out unscathed, but we met heavy weather off the Isle of Man and pulled in for the night. For some reason we found the ship was leaking, but no more than the engine room pump could cope with. We had continual problems with the engines, generally due to water in the fuel, which meant the fuel system had to be dismantled and drained; and the brass nuts on the pipes got badly rounded by the use of adjustable spanners.

We had turned the corner into the Channel when an E-boat suddenly appeared at night. We were steaming in two columns of six and an E-boat sailed at high speed between the two lines firing at the craft on either side. We were completely unprepared; the oerlikon guns were covered and there was no way we could use them without hitting our fellow craft, and it was not until the E-boat got ahead of us that we were able to give it a few bursts from our oerlikons. This taught me a lesson, for we had been completely unprepared for the attack, and had no warning that such an event could take place.

However, we entered Dartmouth and moored up, and were amazed at the mass of landing craft and other ships that had congregated there. We realised that D-Day was not far off, and the strictest security was in place, so the crew were not allowed ashore. Whilst they were allowed to write letters, these were in fact not posted until after D-Day.

Security was such that most of the inhabitants had been moved from the area and there were huge lines of tanks, lorries and every type of armament in enormous quantities in close vicinity to the harbour.

It was no secret to anyone that we were preparing for an invasion, and I was sent ashore to get certain stores and equipment which we had been detailed to take. One high-ranking officer was dishing out toilet roll, and carefully noted how many sailors we had on board, the Admiralty ration being three sheets per man per day – 'two to wipe and one to polish'. The army ration, however, was only two sheets; but when I said we were carrying American troops a look of great concern came over his face, for in all the planning that had been done down to the smallest detail he seemed to regard it as catastrophic that an item of such importance as the number of sheets the Americans were allowed per man had not been ascertained. However, I suggested that as we were all very young and nervous that we might need an extra sheet or two. He parted with a case of toilet rolls, which I signed for in quadruplicate. It seemed rather odd that in a few days' time we might be dead, and so much importance should have been put on toilet roll...

I then went to Dartmouth College and picked up the sack of invasion orders. These were handed to me without me giving a signature. I took the sack on board and we were given express orders that in no way were we to open it until instructed. The next order we had was to go to one of the many loading ramps and load Stuart tanks, which were quickly backed on under the supervision of a red-faced American colonel. When we were about to raise the ramp I went back to the wardroom to find the mat on the deck was floating, and we were in fact leaking badly. I rushed to the colonel and explained this, but he insisted we carried on. However, I told him that we would sink before we got out of the harbour, let alone to France, and he had two tanks driven off, thus lightening the load. Due to the fact we were probably the last craft to be commissioned we had done no practice beachings, for if we had carried a load the severity of the leak would have been discovered.

We returned to our mooring loaded with tanks. We also had their crews, who were going to have to live on the tank deck completely exposed to the weather, and chemical-type toilets were provided for them situated on the deck. Our own cooking facilities were extremely limited, so there was not much we could do to help them. They did not complain, they were well-seasoned troops, part of a Ranger Division, and had been issued with K rations, which were concentrated food of various descriptions; the wrappings looked most attractive but the contents were somewhat tasteless.

The next day we were told to open our sack, which contained almost every detail not only of the invasion itself but where we were to go when the Channel ports had been opened and we became redundant, which was to another invasion, I think, in the south of France. The sack contained excellent photos of all the beaches and our instructions about where to land, and a special code that had been arranged for D-Day. The sack contained details of all the orders for the forces taking part, including the softening-up operations which would be carried out by the RAF and American Air Force, and also the naval bombardments from our battleships, cruisers and destroyers.

D-Day Minus 2

June 4th

D-Day was to be June 5th, and we were detailed to sail the day before due to the fact that we had the longest distance to go. The weather on the 4th, even though we were in the well-sheltered harbour of Dartmouth, looked bad, and as soon as we left harbour we realised the sea was extremely rough. I doubted whether steaming against the waves we could survive the journey. Our craft was leaking badly but the pump was just about able to cope. The rough seas stirred up water that must have been in the fuel tanks and there were frequent breakdowns. Heading into the waves caused spray to come right over the craft as far as the bridge, and the whole craft shuddered rather as if we were driving into a brick wall.

We received a signal to return to Dartmouth as D-Day had been postponed until the following day: June 6th. By then we were down to only one engine, and received a tow from a corvette. It towed us far too fast, and to my horror I saw the huge ramp dip right under the water, sending a cascade of water into the tank deck and slopping the chemical toilets around the tanks, and for a few moments I thought we were going to sink. I went up to the bow with an axe so that I could cut the tow rope if I thought this was going to happen again. The deck had self-draining scuppers, so the water disappeared in the end, but I realised that if we dipped the bow under once more we would probably be towed under water. I think this was the most frightening experience I had during the whole campaign.

I found it difficult to remain calm and give my orders without showing any signs of panic. My mouth had suddenly gone dry, and it was only with some difficulty I was able to blow up my lifebelt.

We signalled the corvette to slow down, and they took us into

Torquay Harbour, which was an American base, where we were descended on by an army of engineers. They did the necessary repair work in a most efficient way, without the normal form-filling we would have had to carry out in a British base.

We were all extremely tired and stressed, for although we had blown up our lifebelts, had the ship been towed under it would probably have meant the loss of life of most of us, for when the ship sinks it tends by the suction of it going down to take the crew with it. They were unable to find out why we were leaking so badly and gave us a Pacific pump as a back-up to the ship's pump.

I had borrowed my father's camera and managed to take one good photo of our fully laden craft battling against the sea. We realised now we had to fight two wars, one against the sea and the other against the Germans. Everyone taking part in such an operation is undoubtedly frightened, and the thought of showing that one is frightened is the most frightening thing of all. As an officer, one has to try and look as unconcerned as possible and give one's orders calmly, for if one shows panic it has a very adverse effect on the crew.

We had a restless night, with work being carried out at high speed by the American engineers to overcome our engine problems. Unlike a British dockyard, they did not spend time having post-mortems over what had gone wrong with an engine, and without having to fill in forms, etc., they promptly changed one or two of them.

All of us were tired out and suffering from the stress of the nightmare journey of the previous day. The American troops had been on board for two days and were having to live on the open deck, sheltering as best they could under sheets of canvas strung between the tanks. They were unable to do any real cooking, for the tanks were packed very closely and there was a considerable danger of igniting the fuel and explosives which they carried. However, they bore up very well, and we did our best to supply them with boiling water for cups of coffee.

On our way over, laden with Stuart tanks

D-Day Minus 1

June 5th

As the dawn came up we noticed it was by no means a summer's day, with grey skies and heavy clouds showing. However, the wind had reduced slightly, and whilst we could not see the sea from where we were moored, we felt it would be calmer. It was not possible to sail back to Dartmouth and pick up our original convoy, and slightly later than the day before were ordered to sail behind a convoy that was going to a different beach, intending to divert to the planned one when we neared the Normandy coast. It was an extraordinary scene, a great armada of craft of all descriptions accompanied by escorts, not only from Torquay but also from other neighbouring ports.

We steamed in single line and joined the end of the convoy, generally known as 'tail-arse Charlie'. No lights were allowed or wireless communication, which did not affect us as we had no wireless, and as it grew darker with only the noise of our engines it gave me a rather ghostly feeling. The troops on board were getting what rest they could and appeared very relaxed.

Our cook did his best to keep us nourished with the customary baked beans, tinned tomatoes and sausages, which were known as 'snorkers and red lead'.

Everyone on board had been issued with an emergency light, which was fastened to their uniform so that in the event of us sinking it would be possible to be identified in the water. We all had lifebelts, which were standard Admiralty issue, and had to be inflated by mouth. The Americans had more sophisticated ones which worked off two small bottles, the same as were used for charging soda syphons, and all they had to do was to squeeze the lifebelt in one place and it would automatically inflate.

We were about halfway across the Channel when we saw some lights in the water and realised that a vessel had for some reason sunk, and although our orders were to stop for nothing, being at the end of the convoy we stopped and hauled the survivors on board. They were all distressed and the best we could do was to house them on the deck and give them a cup of tea.

Unfortunately, the leak that we had been suffering from which had been beyond the facilities at Torquay worsened and we found ourselves lower in the water. The engineer endeavoured to start the Pacific pump which had been put on board as a back-up to the one installed. It was with some difficulty he got it to start, and then found that the hoses that had been supplied had been dropped on the deck and had their couplings damaged, which made them unable to be joined. The worst of the leak was in the engine room, so we resorted to baling out the craft with buckets through the engine room hatch. One engine stopped due to fuel problems, which the engineer found quite simple to rectify, as we had been issued with a set of American spanners at Torquay, making things a lot easier than using adjustable spanners and Stillson wrenches.

The loss of one engine, seeing we had three, enabled us to keep up the necessary speed. The sea was by no means calm, but well within the capabilities of the craft to cope with, but when moving between the tanks to inspect the fastenings holding the ramp were secure, as I squeezed between the tanks – which were only about nine inches apart – I could feel my chest being slightly constricted as the ship rolled, which was somewhat perturbing.

D-Day

June 6th

The hour of midnight had passed and all of us were feeling extremely tired, having not had any proper rest since we set off on the 4th. None of the crew or the troops were seasick, possibly thanks to the tablets they had been given. There must have been some on other craft going through the debilitating effect it can have – often making people wish they could lie down and die.

I look back and wonder whether I was frightened at the time about what we would meet on the beaches, but I think the state of tiredness I was in subdued any feeling of nervousness. For some hours there had been the constant drone of aircraft overhead, mostly bombers, and aircraft carrying paratroops, towing gliders behind them. The mission of the bombers was to pulverise the beachheads and bomb the gun emplacements and strategic points inland. We learnt afterwards that due to low cloud base the pathfinding had not been very good, and many paratroops were landed miles away from their landing point, some landed in swampland, and with the heavy gear that they were carrying many were drowned.

Bombing went on in other parts of the coast away from the landing areas in order that the Germans would not pinpoint where our forces were due to land. Nearing the coast, we could see the beach ahead, and could hear the noise of shellfire and our rocket ships, which were pounding the beaches. Battleships had opened up with their large 14 and 16-inch guns to pulverise defences beyond the beaches.

Engineers followed in order to blow up some of the obstacles known as tetrahedra to clear a path for us to land. Small submarines had been waiting over two days to place flags on the beach to mark the landing places.

We saw some of the floating tanks. Many had been launched

far too early, and were struggling against the waves that were almost too much for them, and also the wind was diverting them from their course. Many submerged long before they reached the beach, with considerable loss of life. Some of the small landing craft known as LCPs were overcome by the waves and sank, leaving the soldiers to swim for the shore with all their heavy gear. Many unfortunately drowned. Heavy gunfire was coming from the Germans, and the noise being such it was difficult to make oneself heard when giving orders.

Unfortunately the Americans had not bombed the gun emplacements as planned, again due to low cloud. At this point we left the convoy which had formed up in line abreast ready to land, and proceeded along the coast, giving us a fairly clear run until we came to the beach we thought was the one planned for us to land.

Along with many other craft, due to the strong tide that was running we did not land on our designated beaches.

We were late on arriving and, turning towards the beach, came under considerable gunfire. The tank crews by then had their engines started and we had two of the crew in each of the winch shelters ready to drop the door as soon as ordered. I joined the Skipper on the bridge, who was looking for a good landing place through binoculars. Owing to tiredness and possibly what he could see on the beach, he turned to me and said, 'This is too much for me, Brian, take over,' and collapsed under the chart table. I picked up the binoculars and saw the bodies floating near the beach, some floating upside down, as they must have been carrying more weight above their belts than they had below. As we headed for the beach I realised that we would have to land on top of them, but in no way could we abort the operation. We carried on relentlessly until we beached, having dropped our anchor astern in order to hold us square on to the beach and not drift sideways. The door was dropped, the first tank started to roll off, and the officer in charge standing head and shoulders out of the first tank was shot in the head, dropping back into it. It was probably the first time any of us had been in action, or at least seen someone shot, and it was with great difficulty we hauled him out, the crew of the tank doing their best to help us. There was no time to deal with the situation in the way we would have liked, so we literally had to dump him on the deck.

We learned later that on another landing craft a tank had met a similar problem, and a member of the crew took the place of a driver, who had been wounded, and drove the tank for four hours into action. The tanks then proceeded ashore. Bullets were still flying round the craft and one almost spent bullet, having ricocheted off the side of the tank deck, hit me fair and square on my forehead, knocking me over. As I fell, I hit my head on one of the deck securing eye bolts. For a second I thought the bullet had gone right through, as I felt a pain in the front and back of my head, but I soon realised the bullet had done little damage other than make a slight dent in my skull – not enough to claim a Purple Heart from the Americans! The crew had already started to wind up the door, it being a slow process; a small engine had been fitted to wind it, which unfortunately would not start at the critical moment.

Due to the fact that we were late on landing, the tide was dropping and the craft was well aground, and we thought it best to take cover on the beach in a type of bunker that contained a few dead. Here we were reasonably safe, and planned to go back on board as soon as the tide returned.

This gave me a chance to collect my thoughts. The crew appeared reasonably calm. One or two were shivering and shaking, whilst others held back their nervousness, and so often it turned out that those who shivered and shook and perhaps cried rather than holding it back got away with far less in the form of after-effects. It was pitiful later on to see an officer sitting in the sand making sandcastles, having gone completely out of his mind, and one could not help wondering whether those who had complete breakdowns ever recovered.

The ship had sustained little damage other than one shell that went through the bridge, and fortunately did not explode but left a neat round hole in the armour plating. As soon as the ship started to float again we re-embarked and kedged off, hitting a submerged object. This, we discovered the next day when doing a beaching at low tide, was one of the floating tanks that had sunk with the crew still in it. It seemed sad that they were only a few yards from the beach, and for some reason had not been able to get out, as they were equipped for such an emergency with a cylinder and mouthpiece, which gave them two or three minutes of oxygen to help whilst escaping.

The beach was littered with damaged craft. Some of the LCPs, which had been ferrying troops to the shore from larger vessels, had been overcome by the sea and sunk, making obstacles for the landing craft that would be following up. Pointe du Hoc, where we were due to land, was between the Omaha and Utah Beaches, and we learned later that Omaha landings had not gone entirely to plan and that as many troops were drowned as were killed in action.

Opposition from the Germans started to die down as the troops established the beachhead, but there was still heavy gunfire from the gun emplacements, the guns on the tanks not being heavy enough to destroy the gun emplacements unless they were fortunate enough to get a shell through the slit through which the German guns were being fired. Some of these were knocked out by brave soldiers creeping forward and lobbing a hand grenade into the gun emplacement.

Some of the Mark V landing craft, including ourselves, were designated to work from the beaches ferrying troops and armaments to the shore, whilst most of the LCT Mk IVs returned to England to load up again, which enabled the crews to get some rest and work the ship's normal routine. But this was impossible for us, working non-stop ferrying from the larger ships which were moored off the beaches.

With night starting to fall, we moored alongside an LST ready to embark lorries to be landed in the early hours of the next day. With the noise going on on the beaches it was difficult to relax. This gave us a few hours' rest, the crew being given their customary tot of rum, and the Skipper surreptitiously drinking the bottle of brandy from the medicine chest, which was clearly marked 'For medicinal purposes only'. At this time I did not like alcohol, but on looking back I am sure a good tot of Scotch would have done me the world of good. I did not take any photos that day, as, apart from the fact I was too busy, I felt it would not have been the right thing to do.

The bows of the craft with the ramp lowered

D-Day Plus 1

June 7th

'Resting' was not quite the right word for it. With all the noise going on and the clattering of the ship being loaded, it was hardly giving one the opportunity to clear one's mind, which was filled with the horror of the last twenty-four hours. The crew had stood up to the stress extremely well and had carried out their duties efficiently.

It was a good thing that due to the fact that our craft was suffering various problems we did not have to make the journey back to the UK. It would be wrong to give the impression that all craft suffered the defects that we encountered. It had probably been commissioned last because it had been put aside as being a non-starter, but at the last minute, when the dockyard had commissioned all the others, they decided to get it running. There is no doubt that it was a jinxed craft.

Having been rushed down to Dartmouth we had no time to do any practice landings. We had not had time to get to know the officers in the flotilla in which we were due to sail, which was possibly a good thing, for it would have been more stressful for us if we had friends on craft which had been badly damaged or destroyed. When clearing the tank deck before the lorries were loaded, the crew enjoyed picking up the large amount of K rations that had been left, and also the Camel cigarettes. Almost everyone smoked hard, but found the Camels a bit rough on the palate.

By now the beachhead had been well established, and whilst there was gunfire coming from small pockets of troops and gun emplacements inland, battleships and other naval craft were shelling deeper into the territory to soften up the enemy troops who were being rallied to oppose our forces, with the constant drone of aircraft overhead. We had had little opposition from the German Luftwaffe, and barrage balloons were being used to ward off low-flying aircraft.

We ferried the lorries to the shore, being careful not to beach on a sandbank, for the water beyond it would be deep, so that the vehicles driving off could suddenly find themselves half submerged in water. All the vehicles had been carefully protected with what looked like chewing gum to insulate parts of the engine which would be affected by water. However, in some cases the vehicles had to be abandoned and recovered by bulldozers, which did an excellent job pulling the vehicles to the shore. Here they were jumped upon by engineers, who would de-water them as soon as possible. As soon as the engines had been started they were driven off so that the heat of the engine would dry out parts which otherwise would have given problems later.

By now an even greater armada of ships was appearing, and we also saw the huge Mulberry harbour with concrete structures the size of blocks of flats towed and sunk into position to form a harbour wall, along with one or two old battleships and other vessels which were beyond their sell-by date and were accordingly sunk to do their last useful job. The huge PLUTO pipeline, that was to carry fuel across the Channel, was being towed across by tugs, wound on something looking like a giant cotton reel.

We had made three successful landings, and by now all the dead had been removed from the beachhead; apart from an odd shell or two fired by the retreating Germans, things were reasonably peaceful. However, the beaches were littered with mines and unexploded shells and the remains of the tetrahedra, which consisted of large steel structures embedded in the beach, on which small craft could easily be impaled and larger craft damaged. Some of these had nasty-looking mines attached to them. A workman, who must have been suffering from shell shock or was a complete imbecile, was busy planting mines, still carrying out the Germans instructions. Instead of being taken as a prisoner, he was ordered to dig them up again, and carried on doing this without turning a hair. It was fortunate the Germans had left so many of the mine warning notices in position, and those who had been detailed to pull them out must have felt that discretion was the better part of valour, and made inland as soon as possible when they sighted the invasion fleet.

Landing at low tide was safer than at high tide, and most routes to the beaches had been cleared, the English using Churchill tanks fitted with flails well in front of the tank, which revolved chains at high speed to beat the sand and explode the mines. These were called 'funnies' but were not used by the Americans. Every contingency had been thought of and tanks had been constructed to unfold a roadway in front of them by unreeling mats, should places on the beach be too soft to take the vehicles that would otherwise get bogged down.

When on beaching and kedging off with the anchor, we found it had snagged on an obstacle, so we pulled the cable in slowly and saw we had part of a tetrahedra which had a shell-like object attached to it. We decided the only thing was to haul it in as far as possible, so it was clear of the bottom of the craft, and when we got into deep water without ceremony we managed to unhook it, and were pleased to see it depart between the waves.

The Americans had already established hospital units in tents to deal with casualties, even a tent with a dentist in attendance. The Americans worked with great efficiency; one could not help noticing how one would see an officer carrying cans of petrol to his vehicle, where if it had been on an English beach, one of the ordinary soldiers would have been detailed for the task. The beaches were strewn with food, to which we had a chance to help ourselves, and we gathered many tins of spam, which was a change from Old Mother Riley's Irish Stew, which we had in khaki-coloured cans. Fortunately the leak in our LCT that had given so much trouble was no longer a problem, for every time we beached the water leaked out again. Our next consignment was to unload nurses from an American ship.

The pace never slackened, for it was imperative that all the necessary armaments and supporting gear were transferred as soon as possible, as the success of the invasion depended on the back-up of supplies. By this time we were all so tired that we were walking round like zombies. We had however no news as to how the invasion was going on; no doubt those in England had been able to read the progress in the national newspapers. Our engines were starting to play up, and we spent the second night alongside an engineering craft, whose crew found defects which they were unable to understand, and I could not help wondering whether these had been due to some minor sabotage when we were in Torquay Harbour, the defects designed with some kind of delayed action effects to hamper our operational efficiency.

The mass of vessels manoevring off the beaches, D plus one.

A tank driving ashore. The large trunking on the back to ventilate the engine would drop off when beached.

Leaving the beach, having unloaded

The beach, after unloading

German mine warning

D-Day Plus 2

June 8th

Having had our defects corrected, we next proceeded to a large troopship where, due to the number of troops on board, urinals had been fitted on the decks, discharging over the side. Unfortunately we had to moor under these, and were literally soaked from above, which was more than unpleasant; we were thankful however that they were only urinals. We managed to board well over 100 men. We landed the troops in shallow water, and they were able to wade ashore without getting too wet. On beaching, our anchor had fouled some object so we were forced to cut the cable. When the tide went down, we managed to get a bulldozer to retrieve it. Unfortunately it drove over a mine, causing the driver to lose a leg.

We made one more landing that day, taking crates of food and other stores including some nicely baked bread, with a few loaves disappearing down to our mess deck.

We moored against large barges designed to carry heavy equipment such as drag lines and cranes for construction work that would be necessary as our troops advanced. These vessels were used to transport troops to the beach, being able to carry far more troops than our craft could accommodate, and were nicknamed 'rhinos'.

An American DUKW (better known as 'ducks'); an Mk VLCT and an LCP in the distance

An LCI, heavily damaged

The beach where we landed – tetrahedra can be seen littering the beach.

Landing craft, known as 'rhinos', for carrying heavy machinery

D-Day Plus 3

June 9th

We had moored alongside a merchant ship for the night, unloading more stores by subdued lighting, when a German plane dropped a bomb right through the hold. I think it blew the bottom out of the vessel. We were ordered to leave at once, for there was nothing we could do to assist the wounded, as there were rescue craft with facilities for such an emergency. The ship had been moored in fairly shallow water and did not completely submerge.

We had seen little of the German Luftwaffe other than on the night of D-Day itself, and during one or two 'hit and run' raids. We were all in such a state of tiredness that we decided to anchor for the night, as we were now reaching the stage when we could not have carried on for much longer without a rest. We hadn't even a chance to wash and shave, for the soot that came out of the galley chimney, which was just in front of the bridge, blackened our faces and bit hard into the skin.

I found it difficult to sleep and my mind was still going through the horrors of D-Day. However, I must have slept, for in the middle of the night the quartermaster found me on the deck bawling out orders to an empty deck and hastily led me back to the wardroom. This gave me a terrible shock, as I thought I was going out of my mind, and for the rest of the time I was on board I always kept the light on in the wardroom, for what reason I do not know.

We weighed anchor after breakfast, having been instructed to unload jeeps and lorries from a troopship. These were lifted by crane, and manned by troops equipped and ready to move to the battle front. We beached on a sandbank and the jeeps drove off, but after a few yards found the water deeper than expected. However, they managed to make the shore without their engines stalling.

We carried out this operation twice, being careful with the second load to avoid beaching on the sandbank.

We all felt considerably fitter having had one reasonable night's rest. Tiredness was a thing that I had never suffered before to such extremes, and whilst Benzedrine tablets had helped to keep one going, they left one with a dreadful hangover when the effects had worn off. We moored that night to a merchant ship that was carrying engineering equipment.

Loading American jeeps

The merchant ship sinking, which we had been alongside

A craft for repairing small tugs

A jeep driving ashore in rather deep water

D-Day Plus 4

June 10th

Our night was by no means peaceful, for whilst we did not have to help in the loading, the noise of vehicles and crates being craned on to the deck made sleep almost impossible. The engineering lorries were beautifully fitted out, with all the tools etc. needed to repair tanks and other vehicles, and the crates contained spares, everything from new tracks for tanks to tyres for lorries. We beached successfully, and with the tide going down and the time that was needed to unload all the crates, we were given our first chance to walk around and stretch our legs. This was the first opportunity we had of being able to have a look round and see what was going on ashore, being extremely careful where we trod, for the beach was littered with shells that had failed to explode and mines that had not gone off.

The Americans were printing the Stars and Stripes and the troops had rigged up some washing facilities, which consisted of a cold shower. We were surprised to see that they had been receiving mail from home every day, which also included parcels. How sad it was no attempt had been made to arrange for mail to be sent to the British crews. It is true to say that you can take a sailor to hell and back providing he has his mail, his rum and his tobacco. We were however given a chance to write home to tell our folks we were still alive on a specially prepared photocopy-type letter which, when it arrived, was joyfully received by our worried parents. Due to the young age of the crew I think only the engineer was married.

By now a considerable amount of German prisoners were being held on the beach. One German officer engaged in a dispute with one of the Americans received the end of a bayonet to stop his nonsense. The prisoners were a mixed bunch; some of them were Russians who had been forced into the German army and were ill equipped, probably to be used as canon fodder. There were a considerable number of very young Germans, no doubt part of the Hitler Youth Brigade, who looked sad and bewildered. The officers, however, were real Nazi types, arrogant and pulling rank when they were not separated from the more humble soldiers. The prisoners were herded on to a landing craft in order to take them to prison camps in England. One officer objected to wading out, and to show his annoyance took off his trousers. It must have been an uncomfortable ride back to the UK, for they were on the open deck of a Mark IV LCT and must have had to stand most of the way.

The unloading went on until nightfall, so we remained on the beach for the night, hoping for it to be a quiet one in order to get some sleep. However, this was not to be, and the biggest air raid that we had so far encountered took place, and the Americans opened up with everything they had. Whilst I could not see what they were aiming at, they seemed somewhat trigger-happy, rifles and even revolvers were being fired into the air, the danger being not so much the bombs but the amount of spent bullets and shrapnel raining down on us. Though I had been in the London Blitz I had never before seen so much anti-aircraft fire. The noise was deafening, and reminded me of the firework displays they used to have at the Crystal Palace. When the dawn broke I could see that little damage had been done, but we had certainly had a very disturbed night.

German prisoners being marched onto an LCT

An LST sinking

D-Day Plus 5

June 11th

We were ordered to sail a few miles down the coast to the Omaha Beach and we noticed how the Mulberry harbour was progressing. Large floating piers with four legs formed pier heads, the legs securing them in position, and the whole structure, rising and falling with the tide, supported floating roadways leading to the beaches, so that the larger ships could unload in deeper water straight onto the floating roadways. In this way their cargoes could be driven onto the beach without getting wet. This was a far quicker way of unloading vessels than unloading into the smaller landing craft in which we were engaged, eliminating what one might term 'double handling' and also problems encountered with the tides. We steamed around waiting for further orders and were sent to a British merchant ship, where we were loaded with crates of supplies, all of which were noted by one official on a clipboard. For some reason they had been ordered to dispense cans of diesel oil to landing craft, but as we had a large fuel capacity, we declined this. In order to keep their books straight they threw the cans over the side, which, being filled with diesel oil, floated and caused considerable damage to the propellers of the smaller craft. It was no wonder that Churchill questioned the need for 1600 boffins to accompany the invasion force to keep the books straight!

We saw many American DUKWs – known as 'ducks' – engaged in taking troops to the shore. These had been carefully designed and could let down their tyre pressures when they reached the beach to give a better grip on the sand.

It made a change to land on a different beach, and we could see the high ground, which had proved such an obstacle on D-Day and caused such loss of life. There were far more sunken and damaged craft and we were told that one of the LCIs (Landing Craft, Infantry) had been badly shelled with considerable loss of life.

We preferred taking loads of crates etc., for these had to be loaded onto lorries. At times this was a rather slow process, giving us time to stretch our legs and survey our new surroundings. The Americans as usual were very friendly, and were able to give us information about how the invasion was going and the difficulties they were having trying to secure Cherbourg, so that we could gain a proper port. Even when captured, it would be a task for our engineers to clear the ships that had been sunk to make it unusable. They told me how there were panic stations when a shell landed at a cheese factory at Caen, the smell from which made them think it was the Germans using poison gas. It was almost dark when we kedged off the beach and moored alongside another merchant ship to unload medical supplies and ambulances.

The beach, showing the high ground behind

D-Day Plus 6

June 12th

We had a quiet night moored alongside a vessel that was carrying equipment for the engineers. It had been anticipated that the Germans would sabotage railway lines, bridges and phone cables, etc. Due to the size of some of the steelwork the unloading was not carried out in the dark, so we had a reasonable night's sleep and again quite a long wait on the beach while everything was unloaded. There was no doubt that the whole invasion had been organised down to the smallest detail, and it was surprising to see sacks of coal, fortunately well packed, which might have been needed if they managed to get any trains running again. We managed to scrounge some self-heating cans of soup which made a welcome addition to our meagre rations. Having no refrigerator, we were existing on tinned food, mostly sausages, corned beef, tomatoes and beans.

Whilst we had little variety in our food, we certainly had variety in the cargoes that we had to carry to the shore. We managed to do a second load that day, and we were given instructions in future to ferry vehicles to the floating roadways which were now almost complete, it not being practical to moor some of the ships alongside the pier heads due to their size, and also the fact that fairly heavy tides were running. We anchored for the night.

D-Day Plus 7–D-Day Plus 12

June 13th–18th

For the next few days we carried on doing two and sometimes three loads to the floating roadways, but on the 17th were detailed to go alongside a vessel carrying ammunition, which was loaded with great care, each shell having to be carried by hand, it being contained or at least protected by laths of wood. This was done with great care, for if one had been dropped with the pointed end downwards, it could well have been exciting! Large crates of ammunition or machine guns, mortars and rifles, took up most of the deck. When we landed, one American said, 'If you get hit tonight, buddy, it's not a lifebelt you'll need but a goddamn parachute!'

A lorry drove on the ramp and suddenly the stern lifted and then dropped, causing the craft to break its back. The deck itself did not split but we realised that the poor old craft had just about met its sell-by date. Unloading went on all night and we could not help but wonder if this was to be our last load. Possibly we could carry on, but only with light loads.

Our craft, showing its broken back

Loaded with ammunition

D-Day Plus 13

19th June

Whilst it was known ashore that we had broken our back, we had received no orders. It would have been sensible if we had been told to remain on the beach and abandon our craft. All the time we had been operating we had received no weather forecasts, and by now the headquarters ashore should have received the warning that severe weather conditions were imminent. We decided to leave the beach with the thought that someone might require our services, but with its back broken our LCT's bow was much lower than usual, thus making the craft less seaworthy; in fact, even at slow speed we were proceeding like a ruptured crab.

The wind was starting to freshen, and as we knew the beach we were on was more exposed than the one on which we originally landed, we proceeded slowly in that direction, hoping that when we arrived we could still serve some useful purpose. We were quite capable of landing troops or anything that was not too heavy. The wind was increasing all the time and we noted many small craft starting to struggle against the waves. We signalled the shore for further orders, and we were told to shelter against one of the huge concrete caissons that formed the Mulberry harbour. The waves were by then increasing in height and we suddenly heard a rasping sound and noted that a crack had appeared across our deck. The gap was very minor, opening and closing only an inch or two as we hit a wave, so we decided to wrap the anchor cable round the craft and pull it tight to stop the hinge-like effect increasing the width of the split wave after wave. We anchored under the lea of a concrete caisson, hoping the rough seas would soon abate.

The storm was now reaching frightening proportions and by midnight the waves were coming right over the concrete caissons which had been designed to give us shelter. By the next morning most of the other craft had decided to beach, and even larger vessels were struggling to stop being blown ashore, driving slowly against the waves and trying to maintain station within the bounds of the harbour. By midday, as our anchor no longer had a good hold, we decided to retrieve it, but due to the fact that the capstan was being used by the wire wrapped round the vessel to minimise the hinge effect, we had no option but to let it go.

By then the beach was a mass of craft and ships of all descriptions in places two or three deep. Vessels were being battered against one another and we felt our only option was to try and stay afloat by sailing against the waves. By now all the destroyers and battleships had left the area, and some of the larger merchant ships who were at risk of being blown ashore also left the area, and proceeded into the Channel where they had plenty of sea room and slightly less rough conditions, for the sea is always rougher near the beach than in mid-Channel.

Our split started to widen, and in order to minimise the hinge effect we inserted the large oak wedges that had been used to secure the tanks on board. However, these were bitten through by the sharp edges of the split deck. The waves were now becoming mountainous, and between each wave we would drop into a trough and the whole craft was engulfed by the next wave. The situation was becoming extremely dangerous, driving everything afloat towards the beaches, and then the floating roadway started to break up. It was driven onto the craft that were now about four deep being pounded against each other on the beachhead. Conditions were such that it was quite impossible to cook, or even keep one's feet. Everything was being smashed to pieces, and we were down to only one cup. The self-heating cans of soup were a godsend, and as for our jars of rum – we had in fact only two – unfortunately they banged against each other and had broken.

By now the split in the deck was so wide that one had to time the jump to cross it, for if one had fallen between, one would have been chopped in two. We managed to keep away from the beach for one day and a night, but realised the craft would soon come in two, both of which parts – if this happened – would probably stay afloat. Whilst we knew that Mark IV landing craft could split in two and retain their buoyancy, we were not sure what would happen with a Mark V. We decided to station one half of the crew on the bow and the other on the stern, the Skipper going to the bow whilst I remained on the bridge. It was evening, and whilst D-Day had been called 'the longest day', this was the longest night as far as I was concerned, for even on the bridge the waves were coming over, and although it was summer-time we were all extremely cold.

By the morning the craft was still in one piece and we realised our only option was to be blown on to the mass of ships littering the beach. Realising that we would be on the outside of all the wrecked craft and debris, and in view of the fact that they were all being lifted by the waves grinding against each other, it would be impossible to make the shore. Those crew who had beached early had abandoned their craft, also those who were blown against those already beached before the wind reached its full intensity had managed to make their way ashore. Being blown against this armada of damaged craft and parts of the floating roadway was worse than we had imagined, for as the waves came in one craft would be lifted and dropped against another with a terrible noise of rending steel, the entire sides of some craft being torn off – including our own, where the side of the wardroom was ripped off as easily as opening a tin of beans.

Omaha Beach, after the great storm

Taken in our wardroom where the side has been torn off, showing another craft alongside (note the electric bulb is still intact).

D-Day Plus 15

21st June

The storm started to subside by the 21st and by then a gap had appeared, enabling us to beach the craft. To see the damage that had been done was quite horrific, and we were thankful that we had managed to get so much ashore for our troops, and how lucky it was that D-Day had not been postponed by a full week, in which case I think the operation would have been a complete disaster. Our crew was sent to a survivors' camp, and the Skipper and I used bits of canvas to make ourselves some sort of a tent on the shore, doing our cooking in a rather primitive way. The Americans generously helped us with provisions.

Such disastrous weather had never been contemplated, so no plans had been made for such an eventuality. We had literally nothing to do, so we explored the German gun emplacements, which had underground passages where those who manned the guns were accommodated. We came across a huge pile of wine bottles, but to our disappointment found they were only full of water. There were stacks of German rifle ammunition, which we noted had wooden bullets. I was glad one of those had not hit me on the forehead – it could well have splintered.

Whilst we were exploring one of these defences we heard an American on the top of the bunker saying, 'There's someone down there, let's throw down a grenade.' In true naval manner we gave them a mouthful of abuse and emerged unscathed. A huge salvage operation was now under way in an endeavour to try and save any craft that could still be operational. Many crews had already returned to the UK, and they were anxious that some would be left to man the few craft that were still reasonably fit. Most of the Americans were still sleeping in slit trenches, and could not understand why we were quite happy in our tent.

Our Craft after the great storm

A tent we rigged up as survivors

D-Day Plus 18

June 24th

We were sent to an American Officers Survivors' camp, and arrived just as they were finishing a meal, only to be told by one of those serving the food that we were too late; but an American officer bawled out, 'Get these men some food!' The food was excellent but we were rather surprised to get scrambled eggs topped with marmalade. We were given the chance to kit ourselves up with American uniforms, but although ours were pretty shoddy, we decided to keep them. However, I did obtain a very fine pair of American boots, which I used years later when back in civilian life. Their lavatory accommodation consisted of two telegraph poles slung across a trench, where one perched oneself chatting to the officer next to one – who was invariably smoking a cigar. This must have been the most public lavatory I had so far encountered!

After a few days we were ordered to return the UK and boarded an LST. I had to share one of the officer's cabins. He did not seem too pleased to have me. Whilst I was only on for about twenty-four hours I did appreciate the American cooking, and also their coffee, which was available day and night. We berthed at Portland in the evening, and were sent to an army camp, which had been a borstal institution; but as we were in quite a dishevelled condition we were not allowed into the officer's mess but had to eat our food outside. I felt this was a poor way to treat anyone who had spent nearly three weeks overseas in terrible conditions, whilst those in the camp had been living in almost luxury. We were detailed to sleep with non-commissioned ranks, which is not even done with prisoners of war. It reminded me how the Desert Rats, when they went back for a short rest in Cairo, did not get the welcome they deserved from those who were enjoying a peaceful life away from the fighting.

I decided not to go to bed, but managed after several hours to phone my parents to tell them that I was still alive. To get a phone connection during the war was most difficult. One had to talk very sweetly to the phone operators…

D-Day Plus 19

June 25th

The next day we were sent to Westcliff. We had a short wait in London, where I phoned my father, who rushed across from his office and managed to have a quick chat with me. We were looked after well in Westcliff. I remember the bathroom having two baths. I soaked in the first one to get rid of the worst of the three weeks of dirt and sweat, and promptly leapt into the other bath for the final rinse. The thing that I had missed most was a toothbrush, and it was a great joy to clean one's teeth. Before leaving Westcliff, we had a formal debriefing from an officer, who asked us if we were all right. We all said we were, for in those days to say one was suffering from stress would have been most embarrassing; there was no question of any counselling being provided or even considered.

We were all granted two weeks' leave. By then some of our beaches had been cleared of mines and barbed wire, and having ordered new uniforms, I joined my parents, who were having a seaside holiday. I found it impossible to wind down and was in fact anxious to get going again and commission another landing craft; in fact it was not long before once again I was on the Clyde actually seeing my next craft being built. It was a Mark IV, on which I later commanded and ended up in Hong Kong, having gone as far east as Formosa (Taiwan).

Landing Craft

There were many types of landing craft, and here I will list a few:

LCP	Landing Craft Personnel
LCV	Landing Craft Vehicle
LCN	Landing Craft Navigation
LCA	Landing Craft Assault
LCT (Mark IV)	Landing Craft Tank
LCT (Mark V)	Landing Craft Tank
LCF	Landing Craft Flak
LST	Landing Ship Tank
LSI	Landing Craft Infantry
LSP	Landing Ship Personnel
LCTR	Rocket ship

LCT Mark IVs, other than perhaps the LCPs on which many of the first troops were landed (the craft being loaded a mile or two from the beach), which carried tanks from the UK, were of greater number than the others. Having large decks, they were extremely versatile, and they could carry almost anything that could be loaded on to the deck.

The LCT Mark Vs were built in America and shipped over as deck cargo on a merchant ship, and would be launched by listing the ship. These were of much lighter construction than the Mark IVs, and I am not sure whether some of them came over in three sections and were then either bolted, riveted or welded together. In later life, having become a marine surveyor, I have often wondered why our Mark V leaked so badly, but the reason could well be that some were brought over in sections, and that could account for it. Whilst smaller than the Mark IVs, they could carry twelve Stuart tanks.

I read in one account of D-Day that these were taken over to France on merchant ships, then launched and loaded with troops. This was completely untrue.

I remember the wardroom when we wanted to hang anything on the bulkhead (wall) we would knock a hole through with a marlinspike and insert a bolt from the inside and lean over the side to spanner up the nut.

It was by no means comfortable living on board an LCT for there was no hot water system. The word 'craft' is used for the smaller vessels, and 'ships' for the larger ones. The following notes that were issued by the Admiralty refer to the details of landing craft, their capabilities, and how they should be operated.

Appendix 1

LOADING OF AN ARMY TANK BATTALION IN LCT MK IV

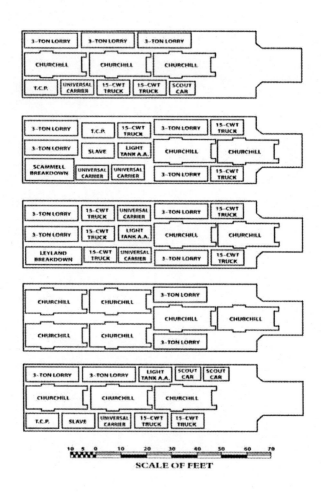

Appendix 2

LANDING CRAFT, TANK
LCT(4). (UNSTIFFENED).

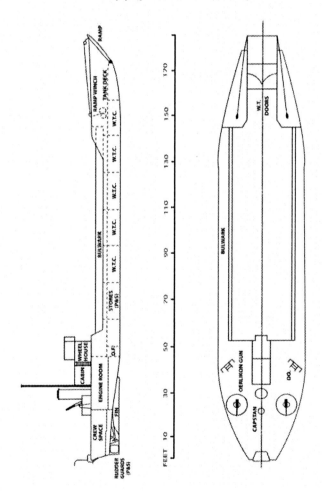

Appendix 3

The Principles of the Preparation for a Combined Operation

1. General Considerations

In the preparation of a combined operation, all considerations must be subordinated to the single object of landing army and air forces on enemy shores in accordance with the tactical plan.

Briefly stated, this means landing at the right time and place sufficient forces to achieve the military object, and following up these forces with reinforcements, vehicles and stores sufficient to maintain them overseas.

The planning of a combined operation takes place in two stages. An outline plan is drawn up by the Planning Staff in consultation with the Chief of Combined Operations. During this stage the Director of Sea Transport of the Ministry of War Transport, the Director of Movements, War Office, and, where necessary, the Director of Movements, Air Ministry, are consulted regarding the provision of merchant shipping and the movements and embarkation of the forces.

After the outline plan has been approved, the Joint Naval, Military and Air Commanders prepare detailed plans in consultations with departments of the Service Ministries and the Ministry of War Transport.

These detailed plans are implemented by instructions which have the joint authority of the Admiralty, War Office, Air Ministry and Ministry of War Transport. Instructions are issued by all these authorities in the mounting of an operation and, where more than one authority is affected, will have been agreed by the authorities concerned and should be acted upon in that spirit.

The success of the operation will depend very largely upon the ships and craft of the expedition being loaded in such a way that troops, tanks and vital stores, such as ammunition and petrol, can be landed in the order of priority required and at a tempo sufficient to maintain the momentum of the assault.

This method of loading necessitates the most careful planning at home and the full and close co-operation of a large number of authorities and individuals, all of whom share at one stage or another the responsibility for the eventual success or failure of the operation.

A mistake in stowage may, for example, result in our land or air forces running short of some particular type of ammunition and so may prejudice the success of the operation.

2. Object of Pamphlet

The object of this pamphlet is to define as nearly as possible the responsibilities of the various authorities concerned with the loading and discharge of ships and craft either over beaches or alongside, in the early stages of a combined operation.

3. Long and Short Sea Voyage

Broadly speaking, combined operations involving assault landings fall into two distinct classes, the long-sea-voyage and the short-sea-voyage operation.

(i) *Long-Sea-Voyage Operations*.—The characteristics of the long-sea-voyage operation beyond the endurance of the Landing Craft Tank (L.C.T.) are briefly as follows :—

(a) Large, ocean-going ships and special ships such as Landing Ships Tank (L.S.T.) must be used, because small ships will be uneconomical or lack sufficient endurance or will be unsuitable in other respects.

(b) All landing craft must be shipborne, *e.g.*, carried at davits, stowed on deck or carried in special ships such as Landing Ships Gantry (L.S.G.).

(c) Owing to the length of turnround, provision of escorts and the time taken to complete the discharge of large store ships, convoys may be several days apart.

In the long-sea-voyage operation some or all of the following ships will be employed to lift Army and R.A.F. personnel, transport and stores :—

Warships	In exceptional circumstances.
Landing Ships Infantry, Medium or Large (L.S.I. (M)) or L.S.I. (L).	Converted merchant ships which carry landing craft. Usually commissioned into the Royal Navy.
Personnel Ships	Merchant ships.
M.T./Store Ships	Merchant ships carrying both M.T. and stores.
Petrol Ships	Merchant ships specially fitted for carrying cased petrol. Capacity, 1,000 to 2,000 tons.
Special Combined Operations Ships.	H.M. ships of special design, such as Landing Ships Tank (L.S.T.) and Landing Ships Gantry (L.S.G.).
Tankers.	
Colliers.	

Note.— " Commissioned " ships are manned by the Royal Navy. Personnel Ships, M.T./Store Ships and Petrol Ships (other than those which are " commissioned ") are manned by their own Merchant Navy crews. These ships, when forming part of an assault convoy, usually have Naval Officers placed in operational charge and may also carry some naval ratings as guns' crews and for other purposes.

(ii) *Short-Sea-Voyage Operations*.—The characteristics of the short-sea-voyage operation, of which a landing on the northern coast of France would be an example, are :—

(a) Coasters, small craft and barges can be employed, thus spreading the risk and reducing the need for employment of ocean-going ships.

(b) Landing Craft Tank (L.C.T.) can operate a ferry service from shore to shore. Landing Craft Mechanised (L.C.M.) may be able to make the crossing under their own power.

(c) Owing to the short turnround and the use of small ships, convoys need not be several days apart. The landing of reinforcements, vehicles and stores may be organised as a steady flow.

Section 3.—LOADING

17. Loading drill.—The drill for loading varies according to the type of equipment, but the following principles always apply :—

(a) The following officers, NCOs, or men will control the loading. They will be detailed by the embarking unit and will co-operate with the normal movement control personnel.

　(i) *On starboard foredeck*—The OC troops, who is in charge of the loading.

　(ii) *In the hold*—An officer or senior NCO and one junior NCO who are in charge of the stowage in accordance with the stowage plan.

　(iii) *On shore*—An officer or senior NCO who is in charge of traffic control and ensures that vehicles are positioned in the right order in front of the ramps.

　(iv) Officers, NCOs, or men who act as guides and are responsible for directing vehicles into the hold of the craft.

(b) A parking area will be set aside where vehicles will be arranged in the right order for loading on to craft.

(c) Good traffic control at the embarking point is essential. The use of tape or whitewash for marking hards will facilitate the positioning of vehicles.

(d) A stowage plan will have been prepared beforehand, based on the following factors :—

　(i) The order in which vehicles are required to disembark on the beach.

　(ii) Tactical loading, which may mean some sacrifice in carrying capacities.

　(iii) The trim of the craft. Vehicles must be loaded so that the weight is equally distributed port and starboard. When it is expected that the craft will ground on a steep beach, vehicles should be stowed so that the weight is thrown more aft than forward. When it is expected that the craft will ground on a flat beach, vehicles should be stowed so that more weight is thrown forward.

　(iv) When stowing vehicles, their wading capacity must be taken into account so that vehicles least likely to drown leave the craft first. In craft carrying recovery vehicles, these vehicles should be loaded to leave the craft first.

(e) As soon as one vehicle is stowed, the next one in order of priority in the stowage plan must be ready to load.

(f) A small party of men should be immediately available for manhandling. An NCO should be in charge of this pushing party.

(g) Unnecessary spectators will not only complicate loading and stowing, but run the risk of being crushed, especially at night. Pushing parties will be ordered out of the craft as soon as their job is finished.

(h) In LCT, Mk 3, " B " vehicles will be stowed two abreast alternatively port and starboard. In LCT, Mks 4 and 5, " B " vehicles will be stowed three abreast in the following order, port, starboard, and centre. See diagram at Appendix B.

(j) The officer or NCO in charge of stowing will ensure that one good fore and aft gangway is left between vehicles.

(k) Vehicles will be secured against movement in the hold by :—

    (i) Wooden chocks and wedges, placed fore and aft under the tracks or wheels of the vehicle.

    (ii) Wire or chain pendants or lashings attached by countersunk eye bolts to the deck plates, or, in LCT, Mk 3, to the stringers running the length of the hold.

Care must be taken to ensure that the vehicle sustains no damage when being secured, the lashings being attached where possible to the towing eyes of the vehicle. The transmission, steering gear, and braking system are easily damaged.

The commanding officer of the craft will give instructions for securing vehicles, but the work of placing the chocks and lashings is an Army responsibility.

18. Details of hold, ramp, and loaded draught of LCM, LCT, and LST are given at Appendix C.

19. **Loading by night.**—Under operational conditions it will be necessary to carry out much of the loading of craft at night.

(a) All drivers will be practised in driving on to craft at night. Some form of illumination in the hold, such as flood-lighting or hurricane lamps, may be used, but this cannot be relied upon.

(b) The procedure for loading at night is similar to that adopted by day. The signals to be used are detailed in Sec 2, para 15.

(c) Four blacked-out hurricane lamps, with light showing only to the immediate front, should be used on each craft to give direction to the guides. The lamps should be placed, two in the after corners of the hold and two in the recesses formed by the watertight doors in the forecastle. The after lamps are re-positioned in front of each row of vehicles as the craft is filled.

(d) Before driving up the ramp of a craft at night it is important that the driver should align his vehicle correctly and centralize his steering wheel. He will then be able to drive straight back into the craft.

(e) Control must be maintained over parties both in the hold and in the area in which embarkation is taking place.

(f) Torches will be dimmed and used on the hards only by guides and embarkation staff officers. Vehicles will not show lights. The indiscriminate use of torches or lights on the hards is liable to cause confusion and signals to craft may be missed or misunderstood. Floodlighting, if permitted, will avoid the necessity for torches or lights.

(g) There will be no smoking on the hards.

Section 4.—DRIVING OFF LANDING CRAFT

20. **Dry or wet landings.**—The slope of the beach will dictate whether craft ground by the bow or the stern. On a steep beach, the craft will ground by the bow and the landing will normally be a " dry " one.

21. On a flat beach the craft will normally ground aft. The landing will then be a " wet " one, and " B " vehicles may have to drive off into any depth up to 4 ft of water, which is the maximum wading depth for these vehicles. Tanks are generally waterproofed so as to wade in 6 ft of water.

22. Drivers must be trained and practised in driving through water in order to get the feel of their vehicles under these conditions. They should also be practised in driving down steep slopes into water, since it is while driving the vehicle down the ramp into the sea, that the greatest experience, skill, and confidence are required. It is at this moment that most cases of " drowning " occur, the majority of which can generally be traced to inexperienced driving rather than to ineffective waterproofing.

23. The following paragraphs, though based mainly on a " wet " landing, are applicable to a " dry " landing.

24. **Procedure in landing craft before beaching.**
   (a) Approximately half an hour before beaching, the commanding officer of the craft will inform the OC troops when the craft will beach.

(b) The commanding officer of the craft will be informed by OC troops of the maximum depth through which the vehicles can wade, if this information has not already been given.

(c) OC troops then orders vehicles to be started up and run for five minutes at fast idling speed. They will then be stopped and restarted five minutes before beaching. No further warming up will be permitted unless conditions of extreme cold are encountered.

(d) Chokes must not be used once waterproofing is completed. Starting can be assisted by placing a hand over the end of the inlet extension.

(e) With the permission of the commanding officer of the craft, chocks and lashing will be removed from the vehicles.

(f) A check should be made of the final stages of waterproofing, *i.e.*, Stages 2 and 3 for "A" vehicles and Stage B for "B" vehicles. With "B" vehicles, special attention should be given to the sealing of breathers and the quick release attachment of the waterproof sheet in front of the radiator (the top of the waterproof sheet should be held in position by a piece of cord with a quick release knot on either side of the windscreen).

(g) Personnel must keep under cover or remain in their vehicles.

(h) An officer or NCO detailed to control the unloading will stand, together with a runner, near the watertight doors ready for the ramp to be let down.

(j) A check should be made to see that all drivers know their landing table index numbers, and the code name of the assembly area to which they are detailed.

25. If the element of surprise is of importance, tank engines should be started up three-quarters of a hour before beaching and run for a maximum of ten minutes. They should not be restarted until two minutes before beaching. On a still night, the tank engine in the hold of an LCT can be heard four-and-a-half miles away.

26. **Procedure on beaching.**—The general procedure for the control of the landing is given in Sec 5, paras 37 and 38. Individual drivers must pay attention to the following points when driving off craft :—

(a) Front wheel drive will be used when fitted.

(b) All types of vehicles must be driven off the craft in the lowest forward gear.

(c) The vehicles must be driven steadily down the ramp until the front wheels touch the ground. Full acceleration will then be applied to get the vehicle moving against the pressure of water ; otherwise wheel spin is liable to occur when the rear wheels touch the ground, and the vehicle may dig itself in.

(d) The driver must keep his foot down on the accelerator pedal, great care being taken that it does not slip off or is not even momentarily raised. This result can be achieved by keeping the foot pressed on the floor of the vehicle. The hand throttle or throttle stop screw will be so adjusted that should the driver's foot slip off the accelerator, the engine will not " die."

(e) Except in fully tracked vehicles, the clutch must on no account be used while the vehicle is moving down the ramp or in the water.

(f) The " choke " should never be used in an effort to obtain more engine speed. The use of the " choke " will cause immediate failure of the engine.

(g) Tow ropes should be shackled to the vehicle or, with hooked tow ropes, these should be moused. Tow ropes will be carried hung over vehicle bonnets. If the vehicle fails in the water the second driver or crew will dismount and hold the tow rope ready for immediate coupling to the recovery vehicle.

(h) Gun detachments accompanying guns must be ready to manhandle their vehicles. Vehicles will carry drag ropes for this purpose.

(j) Every effort must be made to prevent a vehicle from halting in such a position that it blocks the way for the next vehicle leaving the craft.

27. **Points for attention on reaching the beach.**—Vehicles should never be allowed to stop on the water's edge. They should drive straight across the beach (as directed) through the exits to the beach transit areas.

28. Drivers should not normally change gear on a beach until a beach roadway is reached. By changing gear, engine speed may be reduced, causing loss of momentum and consequent bogging of the vehicle or causing a badly running engine to stop altogether.

It is, however, permissible to change into higher gear in the following circumstances :—

(a) On long and firm beaches, where there is less danger of the vehicle sticking, to avoid unnecessary overheating of the engine.

(b) On hard stony beaches which are negotiated more easily in second gear.

(c) On beaches where a higher vehicle speed is required in order to cross strips of soft sand.

29. Brakes.—On reaching land, it will be found that the brakes are ineffective until the water dries off the brake shoes and drums. Brakes should be applied for short distances while moving. Otherwise, if a vehicle is parked with the brakes wet, the brake shoes may bind on to the drums because of the action of salt water. For forty-eight hours after wading, vehicles should not be left with brakes on for long periods, even if " dried out."

Until the brakes are fully dry, drivers must keep at a greater safety distance from vehicles in front than usual.

With carriers, until brakes are dry, considerable difficulty will be experienced with the steering, and drivers must proceed with great care.

30. Removal of waterproofing.—On reaching the beach transit area, waterproofing Stage 4 or C will be carried out. This consists mainly of the removal of Stage 2 or B waterproofing. Later, the final stage of waterproofing (Stage 5 or D) will be carried out. This will include the removal of the remainder of the waterproofing, and for "B" vehicles an oil change and general lubrication, as detailed in pamphlets and instruction books.

31. Landing of motor cycles.—The disembarkation of motor cycles presents difficulty owing to the impossibility of satisfactorily waterproofing these machines. The best method of disembarkation of motor cycles that accompany their unit vehicles in landing ships or craft is by loading them in, or securing them to, the unit vehicles.

An alternative method is to discharge from LCT overside into amphibians or 32-ft Goatley boats, a tubular scaffolding gantry being necessary to lift them over the gunwale of all LCTs except LCT, Mk 4. Light kapok rafts or motor cycle stretchers, which can be carried in the craft, can also be used.

32. Where motor cycles need not travel with unit vehicles, they will be carried in ships and coasters and may be landed by the following means :—

(a) From dried out small coasters.

(b) By trans-shipping into amphibians.

(c) By trans-shipping into landing barge vehicle (LBV) and discharging from LBV when dried out.

SECTION 5.—PROCEDURE FOR HANDLING VEHICLES OVER OPEN BEACHES

33. General.—In a combined operation there will come a period between the landing of the assault troops and the time when the beach is being developed for maintenance, when the maximum effort will have to be devoted to the landing and despatch to their destination of a great number of vehicles.

During this phase, the control organization of the beach group, whose responsibility it is to supervise the landing of these vehicles, will probably only be in process of installing itself, and the routes off the beaches and the traffic control and signposting arrangements, will not be fully completed.

34. **Joint plan.**—Immediately on landing the beachmaster and the beach commander must make a quick appreciation of the situation from the land and sea aspects and decide on the best beaching areas and the exits to be used.

35. To ensure the maximum even flow of vehicles it is essential for the beachmaster and beach commander to have an agreed plan to deal with vehicles as they leave the craft. This plan must be flexible to allow it to meet the many eventualities that occur during a landing operation.

36. The objects to be achieved are :—
   (a) Maximum speed in clearing landing craft, etc.
   (b) Maximum flow of vehicles into beach transit areas, without congestion on the beaches or at the beach exits.

The attainment of the object detailed in (a) above may on occasions conflict with the attainment of the object of (b) above.

With steep beaches, the greatest problem will be to maintain the flow of vehicles into the beach transit areas, without causing congestion on the beaches or at the beach exits.

With flat beaches the problem will be the quick clearance of vehicles from landing craft.

37. **Control.**—Control both of landing craft and of vehicles will be necessary throughout the unloading.
   (a) The control of landing craft on the beaches is the responsibility of the beachmaster.
   (b) Control of the movement of troops and vehicles from the craft across the beaches and into beach transit areas is the responsibility of the beach group commander through the beach commanders.

38. Beachmaster and the beach commander will establish a joint headquarters, just clear of the beach, which will be clearly marked both by day and night. They will issue executive orders for the control of the landing in accordance with their joint plan by one or more of the following means :—
   (a) Loud hailer.
   (b) Visual signals—flag or lamp.
   (c) Runners provided by the beach company or the naval beach commando.

All verbal orders issued by loud-hailers or visual signal will be acknowledged by the person addressed, by raising the right hand above the head.

39. Unloading procedure.—The general procedure for unloading is as follows :—

(a) Craft will be sent in or called in singly or in groups by the beachmaster, according to the requirements of the plan, the leading craft being guided to its beaching point by personnel of the naval beach commando with a " Q " flag by day or a blue or white torch flashing the letter " Q " by night. The remaining craft of the flotilla will keep station by the leading craft.

(b) It is the responsibility of the commanding officer of the craft to sound at the end of the ramp and inform the OC troops if the water is sufficiently shallow for him to disembark his vehicles. It is the responsibility of the beachmaster to provide personnel to sound for runnels between the ramp and the water's edge on flat beaches.

(c) The OC troops is responsible that vehicles are not disembarked at a depth greater than that for which the vehicles are waterproofed. As soon as he is satisfied on this point OC troops will give the order to drive off. Vehicles will then drive off in succession, unless the unloading is stopped for any reason by the beachmaster or beach commander.

(d) OC· troops is responsible for reporting to the beach commander's checker, at the ramp door or water's edge, the landing table index number of the craft load and any casualties to vehicles or personnel.

(e) Each craft should carry a REME flag (blue, yellow, and red) which will be displayed on beaching if the help of the REME beach recovery section is required.

(f) If vehicles stop in water owing to lack of tractive effort or wheel spin the gear should be jerked into neutral and all efforts made to keep engines running until a recovery vehicle arrives. By this means flooding and damage to the engine will be prevented.

(g) As soon as vehicles land, they will be directed by the provost attached to the beach company and by signs to beach exits.

(h) Craft will unload simultaneously or in sequence according to the plan, unless otherwise ordered by the beach organization.

(j) The plan for unloading craft must be flexible. If any delay does occur owing to the breakdown of a vehicle which prevents further unloading from that craft, another craft can be ordered to begin unloading out of turn, so that an even flow of traffic through the exits is maintained.

(k) Once vehicles leave the craft they must maintain an adequate dispersion against air attack whether they are halted on the beach or moving to the beach transit areas.

(l) As soon as the vehicles are clear of the water the waterproof sheet will be released by the second driver by means of a quick release knot.

(m) All movement of personnel across the beaches will be at the double.

(n) Where vehicles are accompanied by personnel, such as gun detachments, the latter will cross the beach on foot ready to assist by pushing. The only exceptions are armoured fighting vehicles' crews, wireless operators, and AALMG crews.

(o) If OC troops has to go inland on the first vehicle unloaded, he must appoint a substitute to control disembarkation. This officer will leave the craft with the last vehicle.

(p) Vehicles will follow the traffic signs through the exits to the beach transit areas near the beach, where Phase 4 or C waterproofing is carried out. Thereafter, they move along the signposted traffic circuits to the assembly areas. In transit areas all personnel remove and dump their lifebelts.

(q) As tracked vehicles damage Sommerfeld and similar track, care must be taken to ensure that they do not drive along roadway or through exits prepared for wheeled vehicles. If unavoidable, tracked vehicles should cross at right angles to the roadway, and should not be allowed to turn on it.

40. The control of the unloading procedure is, primarily, the responsibility of the beach organization. It is important, however, that the units landing should be conversant with the details of the procedure so that they can co-operate fully.

SECTION 6.—DRIVING ACROSS BEACHES

41. **Types of beaches.**—The surface of different beaches varies considerably and drivers should be able to recognize the various types in order to apply the technique necessary to negotiate them. Difficulties that the different surfaces present must be borne in mind when selecting routes and exits from the beaches. There are two main types of beaches : Rock or shingle beaches,
Sandy beaches.

Rock or shingle beaches

42. **Hard stony beaches.**—Hard stony beaches should present no difficulties to vehicles provided that the stones are not covered with slippery seaweed. If the beach is not steep, second gear should be used.

43. Loose shingle beaches.—Provided that vehicles are not allowed to stop and that pushing parties are available, loose shingle beaches are easy to negotiate. Two-wheeled-drive vehicles will dig in immediately unless helped by a pushing party. Bottom gear should be used.

Sandy beaches

44. Hard sand with wet patches.—While no specialized technique is required for driving over hard sand, wet patches may affect the steering Patches of this nature are usually revealed by their colour, being darker than hard sand. Wet patches must be crossed with the wheels straight and without any reduction of speed. Pools should, if possible, be avoided, because their depth and underwater surface are uncertain. If unavoidable, they should be crossed cautiously or reconnoitred first on foot.

45. Hard sandy beaches with strips of soft sand.—On hard sandy beaches, a strip of soft sand may be found along the beach between the high water mark and the exits from the beach. The procedure for crossing these strips of soft sand is as follows :—

(a) A strip of soft sand should always be approached as fast as possible in the most suitable gear for negotiating the bad going ; the gear being changed down before reaching it, and not when on it. Front wheeled drive should always be engaged.

(b) The steering wheel should be held firmly. The front wheels must be kept straight and no attempt made to turn unless absolutely necessary.

(c) If the vehicle does stick, the driver must back out at once. By rocking the vehicle backwards and forwards a firm patch can be made under the wheels which will enable it to be reversed out. If the first attempt fails and the vehicle sticks again, the attempt will be abandoned and the unditching rules applied as detailed in para 49.

46. Soft sandy beaches.—Soft sandy beaches are the worst type of beach likely to be encountered. Unless narrow, it is useless to attempt to rush them as when dealing with the strips of soft sand. Traction on this kind of surface can be assisted by deflating tyres. Cross country pressures as detailed in DME Technical Instruction B400, dated 21st January, 1943, will normally be used, unless otherwise specifically ordered by the formation commander. The following procedure should be followed :—

(a) All vehicles may have to be manhandled until they reach either a hard surface or a prepared beach roadway.

Printed in the United Kingdom
by Lightning Source UK Ltd.
106337UKS00001B/31